RR

SCHOLASTIC

Circle-Time Poetry Math

by Jodi Simpson

NEW YORK • TORONTO • LONDON • AUCKLAND • SYDNEY
MEXICO CITY • NEW DELHI • HONG KONG • BUENOS AIRES

Teaching *Resources*

JEROME LIBRARY
CURRICULUM RESOURCE CENTER
BOWLING GREEN STATE UNIVERSITY

This is for Casey,
who loved counting and charting all the animals
in her Richard Scarry books.

Cover art by Brenda Sexton
Cover design by Maria Lilja
Interior design by Sydney Wright
Interior art by Bari Weissman

ISBN: 0-439-52976-X
Copyright © 2005 by Jodi Simpson.
Published by Scholastic Inc.
All rights reserved.
Printed in the U.S.A.

2 3 4 5 6 7 8 9 10   40   13 12 11 10 09 08 07 06 05

Contents

Introduction

From an early age, children use math to understand and navigate their world. They count their way up and down a flight of stairs. They make size comparisons to choose the biggest cookie. They sort their crayons, game pieces, and blocks into separate containers as they clean up their rooms. They follow simple patterns to set the table for dinner. They count down to holidays and other special days.

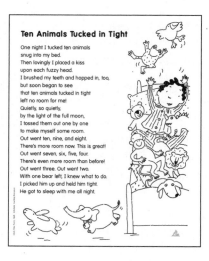

As a teacher, I'm always looking for opportunities to help children develop and apply their math skills in meaningful ways. I've found that poetry is a wonderful way to do this. Poetry can offer students a way to see that math is a central and fascinating part of the world around them. It's in the beautiful patterns on a butterfly's wings, the delicious shapes lined up in a bakery window, the number of candles on a birthday cake.

Children are naturally drawn to poetry, with its rhythm and rhyme and musical language. They delight in the sounds of words and love to say them over and over, enjoying the way a word feels on their tongue. In my classroom, poems serve as "hooks" to bring children together in joyful and creative ways. Choosing poems with math themes helps me make the most of valuable teaching time. The poems do double duty, enabling me to build literacy *and* numeracy and mathematical reasoning.

Connections to the Standards

The activities in this book are designed to support you in meeting the language arts and math standards recommended for children in early childhood. See page 8, for more.

But it isn't always easy to find poems that are just right for young children. I would often look through scores of books trying to locate the perfect poems for read-alouds. It was hard to find poems that met my instructional needs and that would also appeal to my students. Sometimes the poems were too long or the vocabulary was too advanced. So I began to write my own poems to share with my students. Now I'd like to share these poems with you and your students. I hope they will lead your class to make its own exciting language arts and math explorations.

What's Inside

This book includes 20 poems to use as springboards for math lessons as well as listening, speaking, reading, and writing activities. I like to introduce the poems to children during circle time. We continue to work with a poem during the course of a week—or even several weeks—so that children can interact with the text repeatedly. As we read a poem again and again, children become more familiar with the words and confident in reciting the lines. They begin to predict which word comes next and can focus better on the details, listening for specific sounds and searching for specific letters.

During the period of time we are working with a poem, I like to include plenty of opportunities for children to respond to it orally and in writing. We also take time to try a game, art project, or other activity that extends or reinforces a math concept addressed in the poem. To help you make the most of each poem in this book, I've organized the accompanying lessons into the following sections:

The Year Goes 'Round

January, the new year starts.
February is full of hearts.
March is windy as can be.
April rains on you and me.
May days are bright and sweet.
June welcomes my bare feet.
July is hot. Where's the shade?
August is time for lemonade.
September school bells start the day.
October leaves all fall away.
November blows the empty trees.
December shines with lights of peace.

Introducing the Poem

Here you'll find ideas for presenting the poem to your class. I always write the poems in large print on a sheet of chart paper. (You could also photocopy the poem pages onto an overhead.) This allows children to see clearly the words, spaces, and punctuation and to follow along as you read. Children can come up to the chart paper and easily point out letters and words. To spark students' curiosity about the poem, I usually draw a related shape around or near it. For example, if the poem is about the symmetrical patterns on butterfly wings, I'll draw the outline of a butterfly around the words.

Use a pointer to track the print as you read the poem aloud several times. Children can chime in when they begin to feel comfortable with the words. You may want to invite children to act out the poem, do a finger play, or clap along to the rhythm as you read. I've included some read-aloud suggestions for each poem.

Talking About the Poem

In this section, you'll find discussion starters to get students thinking and talking about the poem and the math concept it highlights. I want children to tap into their prior knowledge about a subject and to make connections to their own lives. I also ask specific questions about the content of the poem to check students' comprehension and ask imaginative questions to stimulate their creative thinking.

You'll also find suggestions for getting students to interact with the text. You may wish to ask children to listen for repeated sounds or rhyming words. You can invite them to come up and point to capital letters or letters that appear in their own names. You may want to count all the *p*'s or *b*'s in a poem, underline action words, point out similar spelling patterns, and so on. If you laminate the chart paper, you can use wipe-off markers to underline or circle specific letters or words. Otherwise, you can simply place self-sticking notes under the letters or words that you wish to highlight.

Working With Words

This section includes ideas for simple games and activities to give students additional practice with some of the sounds, letters, and words featured in the poems. For example, if my students and I read a poem that includes several words from the *-ock* word family, I'll introduce a rhyming game to extend the learning. If we read a poem that includes many words beginning with the letter *m*, we might make up silly alliterative sentences featuring the /m/ sound. If a poem includes a lot of action-words, we might play a game of action-word charades. I've tried to include a variety of ideas from which you can choose and adapt according to your instructional needs and students' levels of ability.

Shared Writing

I like to use the poems as springboards to group writing activities. Together, my students and I create simple list poems, word webs, and charts. Or we may complete sentence frames or write a collaborative class book. I want children to connect with the content of a poem by sharing their own experiences, observations, or knowledge about a topic. As students dictate, I write their ideas on the chalkboard or chart paper, sounding out each letter. This is a chance to model the writing process—to show children that letters represent sounds, that words represent ideas, and that writing proceeds from top to bottom and left to right. But most important, it's a chance to give form to children's own words and thoughts. My students get a kick out of watching me write what they are saying. It's powerful to "see" language on paper, especially for young children.

Extending the Poem

I always follow a poem with an activity that gives children some hands-on experience with a particular math concept. For example, if we read a poem about patterns, we might make necklaces by stringing patterns of colored cereal. A poem about mixing up a snack might lead to a cooking activity that gives children a chance to measure ingredients. An art project featuring cookie-cutter shape prints is a natural follow-up to a poem about the shapes we find in a bakery.

Literature Links

This section provides reading suggestions that tie in nicely with a poetry selection. I've included many nonfiction titles that offer additional information about a particular math concept. I've also included works of fiction to engage children's imagination.

Reproducible Poems

Each lesson includes a reproducible copy of the poem. Students enjoy having their own copies of the poems so they can color the illustrations and take a closer look at the words. You may want to provide children with copies of the poems *after* you've introduced the poem to the entire class during read-aloud time. As you model reading for children and point out various phonological elements, you'll want all eyes focused on what you are doing. Later, when you reread the poem and continue exploring the poem's sounds, letters, and words, you can provide children with individual copies. That way students can circle and underline the letters and words on the handouts that you highlight on chart paper.

I also make a habit of sending home copies of the poems with students. It's nice for caregivers to learn the poems with children. They can then recite the poems with their child while driving in the car, setting the table, or washing the child's hair in the bathtub.

Reproducible Patterns

Reproducible pattern pages accompany a number of the lessons. You can incorporate these patterns into the lessons in different ways. You'll find patterns for creating puppets to use as props in poetry read-alouds, for making counters and other math manipulatives, and for making books and word cards, among other activities. Suggestions and directions for using the patterns are included in the poetry lesson plans.

Connections to the Early Childhood Standards: Language Arts & Math

Language Arts

The activities in this book are designed to support you in meeting the following recommendations and goals for early reading and writing put forth in a joint position statement by the International Reading Association (IRA) and the National Association for the Education of Young Children (NAEYC). These goals describe a continuum for children's development in grades PreK–1:

- understands that print carries a message
- recognizes left-to-right and top-to-bottom orientation and basic concepts of print
- engages in and talks about reading and writing experiences
- uses descriptive language to explain and explore
- recognizes letters, letter-sound matches, and matches spoken words with written ones
- shows familiarity with rhyming and beginning sounds
- builds a sight word vocabulary

Math

The activities also connect with the recommendations put forth in a joint position statement by the National Council of Teachers of Mathematics (NCTM) and (NAEYC). The statement describes a continuum for children's mathematics knowledge and skills development in grades PreK–1:

Number & Operations
- counts a collection of items
- understands "how many"
- "sees" and labels collections with a number
- adds and subtracts nonverbally and using counting-based strategies

Geometry & Spatial Sense
- recognizes and names a variety of shapes
- describes basic attributes of shapes
- uses shapes to create a picture
- describes object locations with spatial words

Measurement
- recognizes and labels measurable attributes of objects
- compares and sorts by attributes
- uses different processes and units for measurement
- makes use of nonstandard and conventional measuring tools

Patterns & Algebra
- notices and copies simple repeating patterns
- notices and discusses patterns in arithmetic

Displaying & Analyzing Data
- sorts objects and counts and compares the groups formed
- organizes and displays data through using simple graphs

Sources: *Learning to Read and Write: Developmentally Appropriate Practices for Young Children* © 1998 by The National Association for the Education of Young Children; and *Early Childhood Mathematics: Promoting Good Beginnings* © 2002 by the National Association for the Education of Young Children.

Numbers All Around

I see numbers.
Can you see them too?
There are numbers all around.
I'll show them to you.
Numbers on my soccer shirt.
Numbers on a clock.
Numbers on a birthday cake
and on buildings down the block.
Numbers on my telephone
and on apartment doors.
Numbers on the television.
Numbers at the store.
I see numbers.
Can you see them too?
There are numbers all around.
I'll show them to you.

Circle-Time Poetry: Math
Scholastic Teaching Resources

Numbers All Around

Introducing the Poem

⚙ Write the poem on chart paper. Write different numerals in different sizes and styles around the text.

⚙ Before reading the poem, ask children to take a look around the classroom. Where do they see numbers? On the calendar? The clock? Someone's T-shirt?

Talking About the Poem

▲ Review all the different places named in the poem where numbers are found. Can students think of other places we see numbers?

▲ Invite volunteers to find and circle the word *numbers* every time it appears in the poem. As a class, count how many times the word is used. Can children think of any numbers that begin with the same sound the word *numbers* starts with?

Working With Words

Roll-a-Rhyme Die Game: Write a pair of rhyming words from the poem on a sheet of chart paper—for example *too/you*. Roll a die and challenge students to come up with that number of additional rhyming words. Add them to the chart paper. Roll again for the rhyming pairs *clock/block* and *store/door*. You may want to choose other words from the poem that children can easily generate rhymes for, such as *see, can, show, my,* and *all*.

Shared Writing

Number Helpers Sentences: Model sentence writing for students by writing the following frame on the chalkboard several times:

Numbers help us _____.

Ask children to think about all the ways we use numbers. What things do numbers help us do? For example, numbers help us tell time, call a friend on the phone, play soccer, find a TV program, and so on. Fill in students' ideas to complete the sentence frame.

Extending the Poem

Touch-and-Feel Number Quilt

Students can use a variety of art materials to make textured numbers to delight their eyes—and hands!

Materials

▲ large punch-out numbers (available from craft and school supply stores, or you can make your own numbers from cardstock)

▲ glue

▲ 8-inch squares of construction paper (various colors)

▲ textured art materials (sand, cotton balls, glitter, tinfoil, sequins, popcorn kernels, colored aquarium gravel, and so on)

▲ tape

❶ Ask children to sit in a circle and count themselves out loud. Provide each child with a punch-out number representing the number he or she says.

❷ Have each student glue his or her number to a paper square.

❸ Children then apply glue to their numbers and cover them with one of the textured art materials.

❹ Ask students to help you arrange the squares in numerical order. Tape the squares together to make a tactile number quilt. Depending on the number of students in your class, you may need to add a few blank squares of colored paper to complete the last row of the quilt. Encourage children to feel and describe the numbers' different textures.

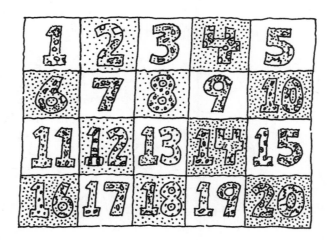

> ✿☜ **Literature Links** ☞✿
>
> The first book follows the adventures of a group of animated numeral characters; in the second book, children count up critters—from one gnu to ten lizards:
>
> *Count* by Denise Fleming (Henry Holt, 1992)
>
> *Rock It, Sock It Number Line* by Bill Martin, Jr., and Michael Sampson (Henry Holt, 2001)

My Missing Mittens

I'm looking for my mittens.
I'm searching high and low.
I need some matching mittens,
but where did they all go?
I used to have a red pair,
a green pair, and a blue.
But I can just find one of each,
and that will never do!
Mittens are supposed to match.
They always come in twos,
like pairs of hands and pairs of eyes
and pairs of socks and shoes.
I guess I'll have to mismatch
to go outside and play
and hope my missing mittens
turn up another day.

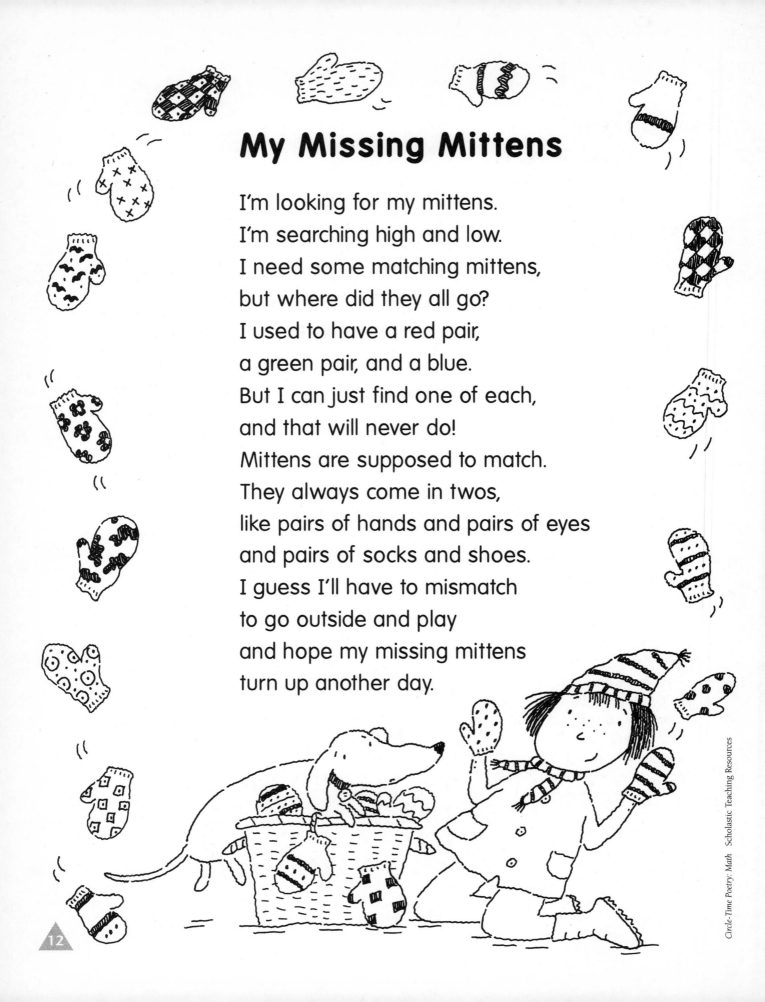

Circle-Time Poetry: Math   Scholastic Teaching Resources

My Missing Mittens

Introducing the Poem

◉ Write the poem on chart paper. Draw a large outline of a mitten around the words.

◉ This poem has a strong rhythm. Show students how to clap to the beat, then lead them in a "clap-along" as you read the poem aloud.

Talking About the Poem

▲ Ask your students if they have ever misplaced their mittens. Did they find their missing mittens? What do they think happens to all of these lost mittens?

▲ Can students explain what the word *pair* means? Guide them to understand that a pair is a set with two matching items in it. What things come in pairs besides mittens?

Working With Words

M Is for Mittens: Ask students what sound the word *mitten* begins with. What letter makes this sound? Together, find all the words in the poem that begin with the letter *M/m* and circle them on the chart paper, emphasizing the /m/ sound as you say the words. Challenge students to come up with alliterative phrases using the word *mittens*. The phrases can be as silly as students like—for example, *my marvelous mittens, my mommy's mittens, my mighty mittens, my munching mittens*, and so on.

Shared Writing

Missing Mittens Word Web: Draw the outline of a mitten on chart paper. Write *Missing Mittens* inside the outline. Ask children to imagine all the places missing mittens might be. Create a word web to show their ideas. See example, right.

Literature Links

The following books are perfect for introducing children to the concept of pairs from head to toe:

How Many Feet in the Bed? by Diane Johnston Hamm (Simon & Schuster, 1994)

Missing Mittens by Stuart J. Murphy (HarperCollins, 2000)

A Pair of Socks by Stuart J. Murphy (HarperCollins, 1996)

Three Little Kittens by Marilyn Janovitz (North-South Books, 2002)

What's a Pair? What's a Dozen? by Stephen R. Swinburne (Boyds Mills Press, 2000)

Extending the Poem

Mitten Match-Up

Students gain familiarity with the concept of one-to-one correspondence as they match a batch of mixed-up mittens.

Materials

▲ multiple pairs of mittens in different colors and patterns (socks can also be used)

▲ box, basket, or bag to hold the mittens

▲ CD or tape player and lively music

▲ mitten patterns (page 15)

▲ scissors

▲ crayons

❶ Have children sit in a circle on the floor. Hold up the box and show them that it contains pairs of mittens that need to be matched up.

❷ Randomly pass out one mitten to each child. Play the music as children pass the mittens around in a circle.

❸ Stop the music, and tell children to look around the circle until they find the person holding their matching mitten.

❹ Ask students holding matching mittens to approach the box two by two. After describing what makes their mittens a match (color, size, pattern, and so on), students can put them back in the box and return to their places in the circle. Play the game again and again.

❺ As a follow-up activity, make multiple copies of the mitten patterns on page 15. Then have students cut them apart and find matching pairs. They can use crayons to make the pairs the same color. Students may also enjoy using the mittens in a game of concentration or in patterning activities.

Mitten Patterns

Fingers and Toes

1, 2, 3, 4, 5 little fingers,
6, 7, 8, 9, 10.
Counting up my fingers
all the way to 10.

1, 2, 3, 4, 5 tiny toes,
6, 7, 8, 9, 10.
Counting up my toes
all the way to 10.

I can count by myself
or count with a friend,
counting fingers and toes
all over again.

1, 2, 3, 4, 5 little fingers,
6, 7, 8, 9, 10.
1, 2, 3, 4, 5 tiny toes,
6, 7, 8, 9, 10.

Circle-Time Poetry: Math Scholastic Teaching Resources

Fingers and Toes

Introducing the Poem

◉ Write the poem on a sheet of chart paper. At the top of the page, draw two hands. Draw two feet at the bottom.

◉ Ask children to take off their shoes and socks. As you read the first stanza of the poem, have children count out their fingers. As you read the second stanza, have them count out their toes. For the third stanza, students should turn and face a partner. Have them count out their partners' fingers and toes while you read the last stanza.

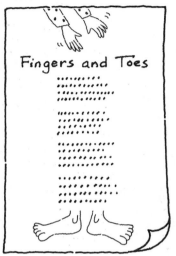

Talking About the Poem

▲ Circle the word *little* in the first line of the poem. Ask children if they can find a word in the second stanza that means the same thing. After they identify the word *tiny*, circle this word as well. Then invite a volunteer to find and circle both of these words in the last stanza of the poem. Can students think of other words that mean the same as *little* and *tiny*?

▲ Use sticky notes, trimmed to size, to cover the initial consonant or consonant cluster in several words in the poem. For example, cover the *f* in *fingers*, the *t* in *toes*, the *fr* in *friend*, and so on. Reread the poem and challenge children to provide the missing letters based on the sound they hear at the beginning of each word.

Working With Words

Number Word Match-Up: Write the numerals 1 through 10 and the words *one* through *ten* on separate index cards. Use the cards in a game of Concentration to give students practice matching each numeral with the corresponding number word.

Shared Writing

Fingers-and-Toes Word Webs: Ask students to think of all the things they can do with their fantastic fingers and terrific toes besides counting them. Make two word webs to show their ideas.

Literature Links

Here are some colorful and fun books that will give students further practice counting from 1 to 10:

Piggies by Audrey Wood (Voyager, 1995)

Tea for Ten by Lena Anderson (R & S Books, 2000)

Ten Apples Up on Top by Theo LeSeig (Random House, 1976)

Extending the Poem

Handprints to Count On

Children will enjoy counting and numbering the fingers on their own handprints.

Materials

▲ newspaper
▲ art paper
▲ finger paint (various colors)
▲ paintbrushes
▲ soap
▲ water
▲ paper towels
▲ markers

❶ Cover the work area with newspaper. Provide each child with a sheet of art paper.

❷ Help children paint the palms and fingers of both hands in a color of their choice.

❸ Show children how to place their hands flat on the paper to make prints. Children always enjoy this activity, so you may want to provide extra paper for them to make additional prints.

❹ Set the prints aside to dry and help children wash up.

❺ Have children choose their favorite print and write the numbers 1 to 10 above their fingers, beginning with the left-hand pinky and ending with the right-hand pinky. Have children then sign their prints.

Yes, I Can
Count Sets of Ten

Yes, I can! Yes, I can!

Yes, I can count sets of ten!

Ten grapes in a bunch.

Ten pretzels in my lunch.

Ten spots on a bug.

Ten stripes on my rug.

Ten children in chairs.

Ten steps on the stairs.

Ten blocks in a tower.

Ten petals on a flower.

Sets of ten! Sets of ten!

Yes, I can count sets of ten!

Circle-Time Poetry: Math   Scholastic Teaching Resources

Yes, I Can Count Sets of Ten

Yes, I Can
Count Sets of Ten

Introducing the Poem

🌀 Write the poem on a sheet of chart paper. Around the poem, draw a ladybug with ten spots, a flower with ten petals, and a bunch of ten grapes.

🌀 Before reading the poem, ask children what the three pictures you drew have in common. Invite volunteers to count the spots on the ladybug, the petals on the flower, and the grapes in the bunch. Explain that each of these pictures shows a set of ten. Tell children you're going to read a poem about lots of things that are sets of ten.

🌀 Have students hold up their ten fingers every time they hear the word *ten*.

Talking About the Poem

▲ Ask students what they think the word *set* means. Explain that a set is a group. A set of ten things is a group of ten things.

▲ What would children like to have ten of? Books? Dolls? Cookies? Puppies? Bicycles? Can they think of a set of ten things that would be small enough to fit in their pocket, such as pennies or jellybeans?

▲ Use sticky notes to cover up the word *lunch* in line 4, *rug* in line 6, *stairs* in line 8, and *flower* in line 10. Reread the poem and ask children to guess each missing word. Provide guidance by pointing out the word each should rhyme with.

Working With Words

cot
cat
pat
pet
pen
ten

Switch-a-Letter Word Ladder: The word *ten* lends itself well to a word ladder activity. Draw a ladder on the chalkboard or on a sheet of chart paper. Write the word *ten* on the bottom rung. Ask students if they can think of a way to make a new word by changing just one letter. For example, if you replace the *t* with a *p*, you form the word *pen*. Write this word on the second step of the ladder. Continue forming new words as you move up the ladder. The words *can, set,* and *bug* from the poem are other good choices for making word ladders.

Shared Writing

Sets-of-Ten Class Book: Allow each child time to explore the classroom and collect a set of ten objects, such as blocks, toys, crayons, and so on. Write the following sentence frame on the chalkboard and complete it for each child as he or she shares his or her collection with the group.

I can count a set of ten ———————————————.

Provide each child with a copy of the pattern on page 22. (Photocopy the page onto heavyweight paper for added durability.) Have children complete the sentence frame and draw a picture of their set of ten. Children then fill in their name and cut out the pattern. Punch holes in the patterns and bind together to make a class book.

Extending the Poem

Paper Counting Chain

Help children visualize sets of ten by making a colorful paper chain to decorate your classroom.

Materials
▲ 1- by 9-inch strips of construction paper (various colors)
▲ tape

❶ Have each child count out ten paper strips in a single color.

❷ Demonstrate how to make a paper chain. Tape the ends of one strip together to make a link; loop another strip through the first link and tape the ends together to create a second link, and so on.

❸ Link students' individual chains together to make one long chain. You will need to untape the last link in each small chain to loop it through the first link in the next chain. Put different colored chains next to one another so that each set of ten links stands out.

❹ Hang the chain in your classroom. Children can use the chain to practice counting to ten and by tens.

Literature Links

These stories offer a glimpse of two entertaining sets of ten—a litter of baby armadillos and a troop of energetic monkeys, respectively:

Ten by Vladimir Radunsky (Viking, 2002)

Ten Monkey Jamboree by Dianne Ochiltree (McElderry, 2001)

Class Book Pattern

Name _____

I can count a set of ten _____.

Marching, Munching Ants

I was sitting on a blanket
eating up my lunch
when along came five ants
to munch, munch, munch.
Then two more marched over.
Count on! Six and seven.
Four more came crawling.
Count on! Eight, nine, ten, eleven.
Three friends followed.
Count on! Twelve, thirteen, fourteen,
marching left and right,
gathering morsels for their queen.
I spied one more ant.
Count on! Fifteen, wow!
I'm tired of these critters.
Let's shake the blanket now.
Finally, those pesky ants
marched off on tiny feet.
They snatched up every snack in sight
and left me only crumbs to eat.

Marching, Munching Ants

Introducing the Poem

◉ Write the poem on a sheet of chart paper. Leave space around the poem so that you can draw 15 ants later.

◉ For fun, spread a blanket on the floor and invite students to sit in a circle around it. Place a basket and toy food on the blanket. Tell children to pretend they are on a picnic.

◉ For another reading, invite children to stand up and march in place as if they are hungry ants coming to join the feast.

Talking About the Poem

▲ Have any of your students ever gone on a picnic? Ask them to share their experiences. What little critters besides ants might want to come join a picnic?

▲ Read the poem again. This time, pause to draw on the chart paper each group of marching ants specified in the poem and model how to count on. For example, after reading line 3, draw five ants. After line 5, draw two more ants. Show children how to count on from five to find out how many ants are now at the picnic. Continue to read the poem, draw ants, and count on until you reach the last line.

▲ Draw students' attention to alliterative phrases such as *Marching, Munching; came crawling; friends followed;* and *snatched up every snack in sight.* What sounds do they hear repeated? What letters make these sounds?

▲ Together, search for and circle the many action words in the poem. Invite children to act out some of these words such as *march, munch, crawl, shake, snatch,* and so on.

Working With Words

Action Word Charades: As a class, brainstorm more action words. Write each word on an index card. Write some of the action words from the poem on index cards, too. Put all of the cards in a bag. Check that there are the same number of cards as students in the class. Have each child pick a card and act out the action. Can other students guess the word? Continue playing until all students have had a chance to act out a word.

Shared Writing

ABC Picnic Menu: What did those pesky ants eat on their picnic? Make a menu and write it as a list on a sheet of chart paper. Challenge children to begin each item with a letter of the alphabet—for example: Provide help for challenging letters such as *q, x, y,* and *z.* Examples might include: *quick bread, xigua* (the Chinese word for "watermelon," pronounced SHE-gwah), and *yogurt.*

> **A**pples
> **B**ananas
> **C**arrots
> **D**oughnuts
> **E**ggplant
> **F**rench fries
> **G**ranola
> **H**am
> **I**ce cream

Extending the Poem

A PleasANT Picnic

Children practice counting on as they tally the ants attending a pretend classroom picnic.

Materials

▲ ant patterns (page 26)
▲ scissors
▲ large paper plates
▲ checkered tablecloth (optional)
▲ dry erase board and markers (optional)

❶ Make multiple copies of the ant patterns. Cut the ants apart.

❷ Spread the tablecloth on the floor as if it's a picnic blanket and invite children to sit around it. Place a plate on the tablecloth in front of each child.

❸ Place 15 ants next to each child's plate. Create simple problems for children to solve using the ants as counters. For example, tell them that there are five ants at a picnic. Have them count out five ants and place them on their plate. Then tell students that three ant friends come to join the five ants. Have children count out three more ants. They should then place these ants on their plate, counting on from five. Ask, "How many ants are at the picnic now?"

❹ Continue posing and solving simple problems in this way. You may want to write each problem as a number sentence on a dry erase board.

📖 **Literature Links** 📖

Here are some other stories that explore math concepts and feature pesky picnic invaders:

The 512 Ants on Sullivan Street by Carol A. Losi (Cartwheel, 1997)

One Hundred Hungry Ants by Elinor J. Pinczes (Houghton Mifflin, 1999)

Ant Patterns

Ten Animals Tucked in Tight

One night I tucked ten animals
snug into my bed.
Then lovingly I placed a kiss
upon each fuzzy head.
I brushed my teeth and hopped in, too,
but soon began to see
that ten animals tucked in tight
left no room for me!
Quietly, so quietly,
by the light of the full moon,
I tossed them out one by one
to make myself some room.
Out went ten, nine, and eight.
There's more room now. This is great!
Out went seven, six, five, four.
There's even more room than before!
Out went three. Out went two.
With one bear left, I knew what to do.
I picked him up and held him tight.
He got to sleep with me all night.

Moon and Star Patterns

Flies for Supper

Frog's long tongue is sticky like glue,
all covered with icky saliva goo.
Out it stretches, zippity-zip,
snatching four flies in one quick flick.
Frog catches three more.
Oh how yummy!
Now there are seven flies
inside his tummy.
There go two more! How many is that?
Nine delicious flies, making frog fat.
Time for dessert. One fly is enough.
Ten tasty flies! Frog is finally stuffed.

Flies for Supper

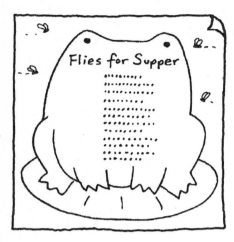

Introducing the Poem

○ Draw the simple outline of a frog on a sheet of chart paper. Write the poem on the frog's belly. Draw a few flies around the frog.

○ Ask children to crouch down and pretend they are hungry frogs trying to catch some flies for supper. Tell them that every time they hear you read a number word, they should quickly flick their tongue in and out and rub their belly.

Talking About the Poem

▲ Discuss some of the more difficult vocabulary in the poem such as *saliva, snatching,* and *flick*.

▲ Ask students what sound the words *frog* and *flies* begin with. What letter makes this sound? Together, find all the words in the poem that begin with the letter *f*, and circle them in the poem. Emphasize the /f/ sound as you say each word aloud.

▲ There are three addition problems in this poem. Use sticky notes to cover up the answer to each problem: *seven* in line 7, *nine* in line 10, and *ten* in line 12. On a dry erase board, write simple number sentences that correspond with the addition problems as you encounter them in the poem. Challenge students to solve the problems before you lift the sticky notes to reveal the answers. You may want to make enlarged photocopies of the fly patterns on page 35, cut the individual flies apart, and let children use them as counters to help them solve the problems.

Working With Words

Initial Consonant Frog Hop: Find pictures of different objects and animals that begin with the letter *f* (for example, *frog, fly, fan, feather, fish, fire, fruit, flag, finger, flower*). Glue these pictures to index cards. Find pictures of things that do not begin with the letter *f*, and glue these to index cards as well. Show students each picture and say the word, emphasizing the beginning sound. Mix up the picture cards and place them faceup in the center of the circle. Have children take turns pretending to be frogs, hopping to the center of the circle, and snatching up a picture card that shows something beginning with the /f/ sound. (Note: You may need to include duplicates of some objects or animals to make sure there are enough picture cards featuring the /f/ sound for each child.)

Shared Writing

Frog Word Webs: Create two separate word webs showing what students know about frogs and what they would like to find out about them. Share books about frogs (see Literature Links, right) to help students answer some of their questions.

Extending the Poem

Insect Snatch-Up

Students help frogs catch flies for their supper in this simple addition game.

Materials

- ▲ frog patterns and fly game cards (pages 34–35)
- ▲ cardstock (optional)
- ▲ craft sticks
- ▲ tape
- ▲ scissors
- ▲ paper clips
- ▲ pieces of red or pink yarn, one yard long
- ▲ small circle magnets
- ▲ pencils or washable markers
- ▲ dry erase board and markers

① Make several copies of the frog patterns and fly game cards. You may want to copy them onto cardstock, or laminate, for durability.

② For each game setup, cut out a frog and tape it to a craft stick. Then tape one end of the yarn to the back of a frog, near its mouth. Tie the magnet to the other end of the yarn.

③ Attach a paper clip to each fly card. Then spread the cards facedown on the floor.

④ Tell children to pretend that the yarn is the frog's long, sticky tongue. Model how to "catch" the flies by touching the magnet to a paper clip.

⑤ Divide the class into small groups. Let each child have a turn "catching" two fly cards by using the magnet dangling from the yarn. The child then counts the flies on each card and writes the number on the back.

⑥ Show students how to use the cards to write a number sentence on the dry erase board. For example, if a child "catches" two flies and then three flies, write the number sentence 2 + 3 = __. Children can solve the problem by counting the flies on the cards. Continue writing and solving addition problems until each child has had a chance to "catch" some flies.

✦ Literature Links ✦

The first three books explore the concept of addition in engaging ways; the latter two focus on frogs and their fascinating characteristics:

Adding It Up by Rosemary Wells (Puffin, 2001)

Adding It Up at the Zoo by Judy Nayer (Yellow Umbrella, 2002)

Animals on Board by Stuart J. Murphy (HarperCollins, 1998)

Frogs by Gail Gibbons (Holiday House, 1994)

The Icky Sticky Frog by Dawn Bentley (Piggy Toes Press, 1999)

Circle-Time Poetry: Math   Scholastic Teaching Resources

Fly Game Cards

Ten Little Campers

Ten little campers roasting
ten marshmallows on sticks.
Four filled their bellies.
That left just six.

Six little campers
roasting, toasting,
yum, yum, yum!
Five began munching.
Soon there was only one.

One little camper
roasting, toasting hers just so.
She gobbled up her marshmallow.
That left ZERO!

Circle-Time Poetry: Math Scholastic Teaching Resources

Ten Little Campers

Introducing the Poem

🌀 Write the poem on a sheet of chart paper. Draw a border of marshmallows around the poem.

🌀 Before reading the poem, give each child a stick with a marshmallow on it. Have children pretend to toast their marshmallows over a make-believe campfire as you read the poem aloud.

Talking About the Poem

▲ Has anyone in your class ever gone camping? Did they roast marshmallows? What did the roasted marshmallows look, feel, and taste like? Can they remember how many they ate?

▲ Each stanza of the poem contains a subtraction problem. Use sticky notes to cover up the answer to each problem: *six* in line 4, *one* in line 9, and *zero* in line 13. Ask ten children to stand in a line in front of the group, holding their sticks with marshmallows. Reread the poem and have these "campers" act out each subtraction problem. Challenge the rest of the class to solve the problem before you reveal the answer beneath the sticky note. On a dry erase board, write a number sentence that corresponds with each subtraction problem that students act out. (Note: Since the sticks may be dirty, discard the marshmallows. Tell children there will be fresh marshmallows to eat in other activities.)

Working With Words

Phoneme Blending Game: On a sheet of chart paper, write the following short words associated with camping: *tent, camp, pot, hot, yum, log, stick, sit,* and *sing*. Sound out each letter as you write. Then randomly choose one of the words. Without telling children which word you have chosen, orally segment it. After you clearly pronounce each phoneme, challenge students to blend the sounds together and guess the word. Continue segmenting words on the list until students have guessed them all. Follow up by cutting out 3-inch squares from white paper. Round the corners to make them look like marshmallows. Write the letters of each camping word on individual marshmallows. Mix up each set of marshmallows and challenge children to put the letters in order to spell a camping word.

Literature Links

Here are several books that help offer whimsical introductions to the concept of subtraction:

Elevator Magic by Stuart J. Murphy (HarperCollins, 1997)

Monster Musical Chairs by Stuart J. Murphy (HarperCollins, 2000)

Red Riding Hood's Math Adventure by Lalie Harcourt and Ricki Wortzman (Charlesbridge, 2001)

Twenty Is Too Many by Kate Duke (Dutton, 2000)

Shared Writing

Marshmallow List Poem: Create a class list poem about marshmallows. Write the word *Marshmallows* at the top of a sheet of chart paper. Give each child a large marshmallow to eat. Ask students to think of words that describe how marshmallows look, feel, and taste. List their ideas. At the bottom of the list, write the word *Marshmallows* again.

Marshmallows
white
soft
puffy
squishy
sweet
yummy
Marshmallows

Extending the Poem

Marshmallow Math

Here's a lesson in subtraction that's good enough to eat!

Materials

▲ paper plates
▲ bag of mini-marshmallows
▲ dry erase board and markers
▲ small paper cups or napkins

1 Work with two to three children at a small group station. Give each child a paper plate with ten marshmallows on it.

2 Model a simple subtraction problem using extra marshmallows. For example, "I brought ten marshmallows on my camping trip. I ate three. How many did I have left?" Demonstrate how to take away—or *subtract*—three marshmallows from the plate, then count the remaining marshmallows to solve the problem. Write the word problem as a number sentence on the dry erase board: $10 - 3 = 7$.

3 Make up new word problems for children to solve using the marshmallow manipulatives. Guide children in writing each word problem as a number sentence on the dry erase board.

4 When you are finished with the activity, throw out the marshmallows that students used as counters. Allow children to take ten fresh marshmallows as a treat. (Check with caregivers for children with food allergies and have a substitute treat on hand for those who cannot eat the marshmallows.)

Patterns, Patterns, Everywhere!

Patterns, patterns, everywhere.
Do you see what I can see?
Patterns here and patterns there.
Come along and look with me.
Day and night,
dark and light,
trading places in the sky.
Spots and lines,
bold designs,
insect wings
catch my eye.
Seasons flow,
come and go,
taking turns throughout the year.
Yellow and red,
a flower bed,
blooming tulips bring us cheer.
Patterns, patterns, everywhere.
Do you see what I can see?
Patterns here and patterns there.
Come along and look with me.

Circle-Time Poetry: Math   Scholastic Teaching Resources

Patterns, Patterns, Everywhere!

Patterns, Patterns, Everywhere!

Introducing the Poem

Write the poem on a sheet of chart paper. Leave enough space around the poem so that you can draw a patterned border later.

Before reading the poem, ask children if they know what a pattern is. Allow time for students to share their ideas. Explain that a pattern is something that repeats in a certain order. Along the sides of the poem, draw a pattern using simple icons, for example: heart, sun, star; heart, sun, star; and so on. Use the same icons to create different patterns along the bottom and sides of the poem. Solicit help from the children as you complete the patterns by asking, "What comes next?"

Talking About the Poem

Ask your students to look around the room or on their own clothing for patterns. Is there a pattern on the rug or floor? Do they notice any patterns on the classroom calendar? Are any children wearing stripes? Is anyone wearing a necklace with a pattern of beads?

Spend some time writing out or illustrating some of the patterns mentioned in the poem. For example, solicit students' help in naming the seasons as you write the pattern on chart paper: *winter, spring, summer, fall; winter, spring, summer, fall*; and so on. Use colored markers to draw a simple garden with a repeating pattern of red and yellow tulips. As you write or draw a pattern, ask children what comes next. Or invite volunteers to come up to the chart pad and continue the pattern themselves.

Ask students to look for the many pairs of rhyming words in the poem. Underline each pair with a different colored marker.

Working With Words

Spelling Pattern Word Sort: Remind children that patterns are everywhere—even in words. Try a pocket chart activity to illustrate this point. Choose a pair of rhyming words from the poem and brainstorm a list of additional rhymes. For example, for *see/me*, you might come up with *be, bee, sea, he, knee, tea, tree, three, we*. Write each word on an index card. Place the cards along the bottom of a pocket chart. Ask children what they notice about the letters used to make the long-*e* sound in these rhyming words. Then have them sort the cards into three separate columns based on the words' spelling patterns (*-e, -ee, -ea*). Repeat the activity using other rhyming words from the poem.

Shared Writing

Patterns Word Web: Create a word web showing places we can find patterns. Include some of the places mentioned in the poem.

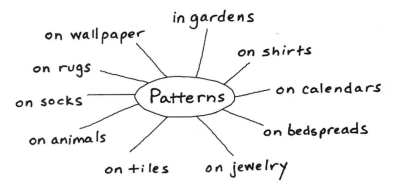

Extending the Poem

Pretty Pattern Necklaces

For a yummy lesson in creating patterns, children make necklaces using cereal.

Materials

▲ colored O-shaped cereal
▲ bowls
▲ small paper cups
▲ pieces of yarn, each 2 feet long
▲ tape

1. Before beginning the activity, sort the cereal by colors into separate bowls. (Provide extra cereal for snacking in paper cups with substitute treats for children with food allergies.)

2. Provide each child with a piece of yarn. Tie a large knot at one end of the yarn so that the cereal will not slip off. Wrap tape around the other end of the yarn to avoid unraveling.

3. Demonstrate how to thread the yarn through the cereal to make a necklace. Model different color patterns for students to create, such as ABAB, ABC, AABB, AABAAB, and so on.

4. Tie the finished necklaces around students' necks. Allow time for children to show their necklaces to the group and talk about the patterns they created.

There are many books about patterns but these are exceptional:

Lots and Lots of Zebra Stripes: Patterns in Nature by Stephen R. Swinburne (Boyds Mills Press, 2002)

Nature's Paintbrush: The Patterns and Colors Around You by Susan Stockdale (Simon & Schuster, 1999)

Pattern Bugs by Trudy Harris (Millbrook Press, 2001)

Patterns by Sara Pistoia (Child's World, 2002)

Literature Links

Bake Me a Shape

Pat-a-cake, pat-a-cake, baker's man,
bake me a shape as fast as you can.
Tasty circle cookies,
sweet brownie squares,
delicious pie triangles
that we can share.
Pat-a-cake, pat-a-cake, baker's man,
bake me a shape as fast as you can.

Circle-Time Poetry: Math Scholastic Teaching Resources

Bake Me a Shape

Introducing the Poem

- Write the poem on a sheet of chart paper. Draw rows of circles, squares, and triangles above and below the text.

- Wear a chef's hat as you read the poem and track the words with a wooden spoon.

- Invite children to play pat-a-cake with a partner as you read lines 1–2 and 7–8 of the poem. When you read lines 3, 4, and 5, children can trace the corresponding shape in the air with a finger.

Talking About the Poem

▲ Ask volunteers to draw some circle-shaped cookies, square-shaped brownies, and triangle-shaped slices of pie on a dry erase board. Can students think of other foods that are shaped like circles, squares, and triangles? What other shapes can children name and draw? A rectangle? A diamond? An oval? Discuss the characteristics of each shape.

▲ Bring in some simple cookie cutter shapes. Have children pass them around the circle as everyone chants, "Pat-a-cake, pat-a-cake, baker's man, what kind of shape do you have in your hand?" At the end of the chant, whoever has a cookie cutter should hold it up and identify the shape. Continue playing the game to reinforce the names of the different shapes.

▲ Point out that the word *shape* begins with the /sh/ sound. Can children find another word in the poem that begins with this sound? Besides *shape* and *share*, what other words can they think of that begin with /sh/?

Working With Words

Pat-a-Cake Rhyming Game: Underline the words *man* and *can* in the first two lines of the poem. What do students notice about these words? Generate a list of additional rhyming words for *man* and *can*, such as *van, pan, Jan, Dan, fan, ran,* and *tan.* Ask children to come up with new sentences using these rhyming words to replace the second line of the poem. For example:

> *Pat-a-cake, pat-a-cake, baker's man,*
> *bake some cakes and put them in your van.*

Have children play pat-a-cake with a partner as they chant each new rhyming couplet.

Literature Links

Here are some excellent resources for introducing students to various shapes and helping them recognize these shapes in things they see every day:

My Shapes by Rebecca Emberley (Little, Brown, 2000)

Shapes, Shapes, Shapes by Tana Hoban (HarperCollins, 1995)

Shape of Things by Dayle Ann Dodds (Candlewick, 1996)

So Many Circles, So Many Squares by Tana Hoban (Greenwillow, 1998)

Shared Writing

Shape Chart: Create a simple three-column chart with the headings *Circles, Squares,* and *Triangles.* Ask children to describe the characteristics of each shape and provide examples of things that are that shape. List their ideas under the appropriate heading.

Circles	Squares	Triangles
round	4 corners	3 corners
no sides	4 straight sides	3 slanted sides
clock	sandwich	pointy
penny	napkin	sail on sailboat

Extending the Poem

Shape Print Art

Students use cookie cutters to make colorful shape print designs.

Materials

▲ newspaper
▲ tempera paints (various colors)
▲ shallow aluminum trays
▲ bowls of water
▲ 9- by 18-inch sheets of white paper
▲ cookie cutters (various shapes such as circles, squares, triangles, diamonds, and ovals)*

❶ Cover work surfaces with newspaper. Pour a thin layer of tempera paint into several aluminum trays. Set the paint trays and bowls of water on the work surface.

❷ Provide each child with a sheet of paper. Demonstrate how to dip the cookie cutters into the paint and press them onto the paper to make prints. Remind children that they should rinse the cookie cutters in water before printing with a different color.

❸ Encourage children to be creative as they make their own shape prints. They may want to make a picture using one shape or multiple shapes, one color or multiple colors, overlapping shapes or patterns of shapes.

❹ Allow time for children to share their designs and talk about the different shapes they used.

*Note: If you don't have cookie cutters available, you can cut sponges into desired shapes, or you can use yogurt containers, blocks, and other everyday objects in familiar shapes to make the prints.

Beautiful Butterflies

Sometimes things in nature
look like artwork to my eyes.
Could it be a painter
has been painting butterflies?
Their patterns are so pretty,
designed so carefully.
Each wing is like the other,
matching perfectly.
They flutter through the garden,
dazzling my eyes.
I run right home to paint my own
beautiful butterflies.

Beautiful Butterflies

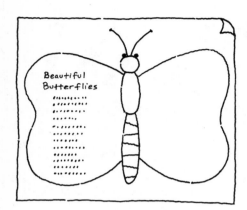

Beautiful
Butterflies

Introducing the Poem

◉ Write the poem on a sheet of chart paper. Draw the outline of a butterfly around the words.

◉ Provide each child with a paintbrush. As you read the poem aloud, invite children to swirl their brushes in the air and pretend to be painters painting the wings of butterflies.

Talking About the Poem

▲ Show children pictures of butterflies in books or nature magazines. What do they notice about their left and right wings? Do the designs look the same or different? Point out that each spot or line on one side has a matching spot or line on the other side.

▲ Have children use their paintbrushes to "paint" imaginary matching butterfly wings. Model how to do this by painting a simple pattern in the air. As you paint, describe what you are doing. For example, you might say, "Let's paint a pattern on a butterfly's wings. On this wing, we'll paint three stripes and two dots. Now we have to paint the other wing so that it's exactly the same." When children are comfortable with the activity, allow volunteers to take turns leading the group in painting matching wing patterns.

▲ Invite children to find and circle all the initial *p*'s and *b*'s in the poem.

Working With Words

Initial Consonant Paintbrush Game: Let children continue their make-believe painting as they work with the letter *p*. Go around the circle and ask each child to name something he or she is painting that begins with the /p/ sound—for example, "I am painting a pink pig" or "I am painting pancakes and pizza." Children can swirl their paintbrushes in the air as they speak.

Shared Writing

Symmetry Chart: Gather objects or pictures of objects that are symmetrical and some that are not symmetrical. Show students the objects or pictures one by one. Which items have matching parts on both sides and which items do not? Chart students' conclusions.

Parts Match Exactly	Parts Do Not Match Exactly
feather	cloud
doll	penny
leaf	rock
acorn	puzzle piece
pretzel	flag

Extending the Poem

Paint-Blot Butterflies

Reinforce the concept of symmetry by inviting children to make butterflies with matching wings.

Materials

- ▲ newspaper
- ▲ 9- by 12-inch sheets of white construction paper (prefolded in half, the short way)
- ▲ eyedroppers
- ▲ tempera paint (various colors)
- ▲ pencils
- ▲ scissors
- ▲ hole punch (optional)
- ▲ string or yarn (optional)

1. Cover the work surface with newspaper. Give each child a folded sheet of construction paper. Have children open the paper and place it flat on the desk. Point out the fold line down the middle of the page.

2. Have children use the eyedroppers and paint to create colorful patterns and designs on one half of the paper. Tell children to drop small amounts of paint and to be sure not to cross the fold line.

3. Have students refold the page and gently rub their hand over it, pressing the two halves together.

4. Tell children to open up their folded pages. Surprise! The blank side of the page is now covered with paint. Ask children what they notice about the designs on both sides of the fold line. Point out that they are exactly the same—just like a butterfly's wings.

5. Help children draw the outline of a butterfly around their painted designs.

6. Have children cut out their butterflies. Display the symmetrical designs around the room. Look for matching parts in each design. Optional: Punch a hole in the center of each butterfly, near the top. Then tie a length of string or yarn through the hole. Hang the butterflies from the ceiling or a clothesline.

Literature Links

In the first book, you'll find an array of butterfly wings captured in stunning photos. In the second book, a brother and sister learn a lesson about symmetry as they build and fly a kite:

The Butterfly Alphabet by Kjell B. Sandved (Scholastic, 1999)

Let's Fly a Kite by Stuart J. Murphy (HarperCollins, 2000)

Patterns by David Kirkby (Heinemann, 1996)

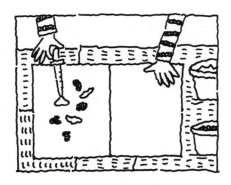

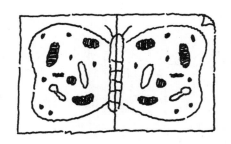

Tick Tock!

Tick tock, tick tock.
Listen, listen, to the clock.
Tick tock upon my chin.
At 7:00 o'clock, the day begins.
Tick tock upon my back.
At 10:00 o'clock, it's time for snack.
Tick tock upon my feet.
At 12:00 o'clock, there's lunch to eat.
Tick tock upon my lap.
At 2:00 o'clock, it's time to nap.
Tick tock upon my ear.
At 3:00 o'clock, playtime's here.
Tick tock upon my finger.
At 6:00 o'clock, it's time for dinner.
Tick tock upon my head.
At 8:00 o'clock, it's time for bed.
Tick tock, tick tock.
Listen, listen, to the clock.

Circle-Time Poetry: Math Scholastic Teaching Resources

Tick Tock!

Introducing the Poem

◎ Write the poem on a sheet of chart paper. Draw a few clocks around the text.

◎ Invite students to tap the body part named in each rhyming couplet as you read the poem aloud.

Talking About the Poem

▲ Ask children why they think we need clocks. How do clocks help us every day? What might happen if we didn't have clocks?

▲ Ask children to talk about the times they do specific activities. Do they know what time they get up in the morning? What time they have lunch? What time they go to bed?

▲ Use a classroom demonstration clock to show the different times mentioned in the poem. Then use sticky notes to cover up each reference to a specific hour in the text. As you reread the poem, move the hands of the clock to show different hours of the day. Ask children to say the time by reading the clock instead of the words.

Working With Words

Word Family Clapping Game: Invite children to join you in reciting the following rhyme as everyone claps to the beat:

Tick, tock. Tock, tock.
Let's think of a word that rhymes with clock.

Call out a child's name and have him or her say a rhyming word. Students can provide actual words or nonsense words, as long as they rhyme with *clock*.

Shared Writing

Silly Rhyming Couplets: Invite children to innovate on some of the lines in the poem by substituting different body parts and coming up with new rhymes. For example, you might write the following frame on the chalkboard:

Tick tock upon my knee,
at 4:00 o'clock, ————————————.

(Continues)

Ask children to help you fill in the blank by providing a new activity that rhymes with *knee*—for example, *it's time for tea* or *we see a bee*. The new lines can be as silly as children like. Other possible body parts to substitute that lend themselves to rhyming are *nose, cheek, hand, hair, belly,* and *leg.* You may want to use students' rhyming couplets to create a new poem titled "Tick Tock!"

Extending the Poem

Tick-Tock Clock Faces

Students make personalized clocks to use as props for a poetry read-aloud.

Materials

▲ clock pattern (page 51)   ▲ crayons or markers

▲ cardstock   ▲ yarn

▲ scissors   ▲ glue

▲ brass fasteners

❶ To prepare for the activity, copy the clock pattern page onto cardstock and cut out the pieces. Use a pencil to poke a hole in the center of the clock and at the ends of the clock hands.

❷ Provide each child with a clock face and a set of clock hands. Invite children to color the clock hands. Then show them how to use the brass fastener to attach the clock's hands to the center of the clock face.

❸ Have them use crayons or markers to trace the numbers 1–12 on their clock.

❹ Tell children that the front of a clock is called a *face.* Then invite them to color and decorate the clock so that it looks like their face. Invite them to draw eyes and a mouth, color the background, and affix yarn hair using glue.

❺ Model how to move the clock's hands to show different times. Then divide the class into pairs and have them take turns acting out the poem. One child shows the time on his or her clock while the other pantomimes the corresponding activity.

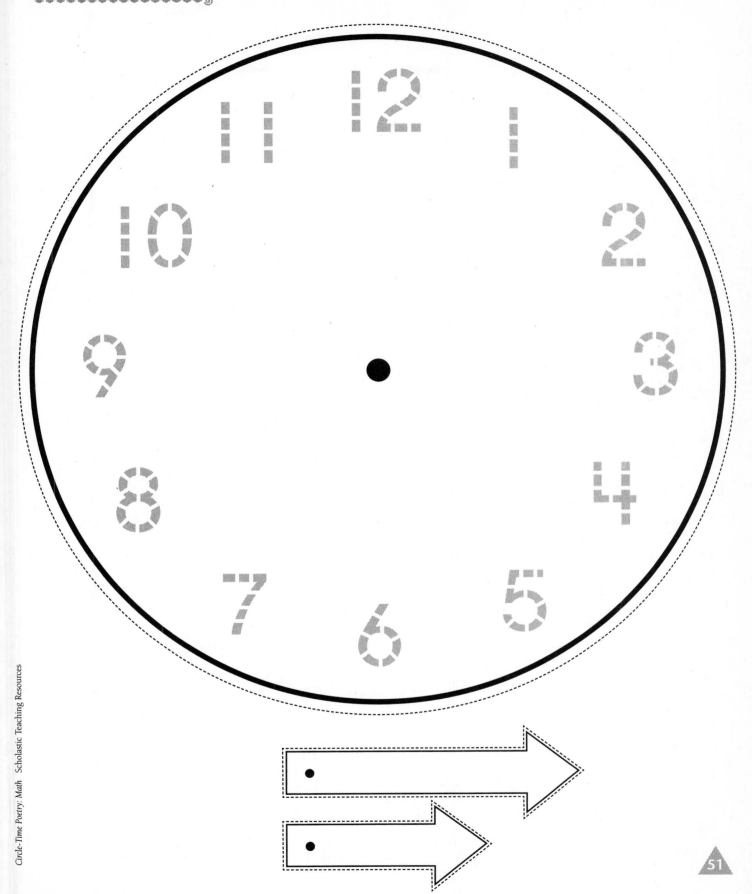

Seven Days Make a Week

I wonder how the animals
in the jungle spend a week.
Let's go to the rain forest
and take a little peek.
On Sunday, the jaguars
are climbing in the trees.
On Monday, the monkeys
are counting all their fleas.
On Tuesday, the toucans
are polishing their beaks.
On Wednesday, the parrots
are playing hide-and-seek.
On Thursday, the turtles
are snacking on the leaves.
On Friday, the boas
are waiting for a squeeze.
On Saturday, the tree frogs
are practicing their leaps.
And all week long, the lazy sloths
just sleep and sleep and sleep.

Seven Days Make a Week

Introducing the Poem

⦾ Write the poem on a sheet of chart paper. Surround the poem with vines and large leaves to suggest a jungle.

⦾ As you read the poem aloud, invite children to pantomime all of the things the animals do, such as climbing trees, counting fleas, polishing beaks, and so on.

Talking About the Poem

▲ Show children pictures of the different animals mentioned in the poem. Provide background information about any of the animals they aren't familiar with (see Literature Links, page 54).

▲ Ask children what special activities they do on different days of the week. Do they have music class on a special day? What day is pizza day in the cafeteria? Do they have soccer practice or dance lessons on certain days?

▲ Review the names and order of the days of the week. Then use sticky notes to cover these words in the text. Reread the poem and ask children to provide the name of each missing day. Offer guidance by asking questions such as, "What is the first day of the week? What day comes after Tuesday? What day comes before Saturday?" and so on.

▲ Place sticky notes under the following words in the poem: *week, peek, trees, monkeys, fleas, beaks, seek, leaves, squeeze, leaps,* and *sleep.* Say each word aloud. Ask students what sound all of these words have in common. Point out the different spelling patterns used to make the long-*e* sound.

Working With Words

Initial Consonant Match-Up: Write each animal name from the poem on a blank index card. Snip off the initial consonant or consonant cluster. Put the cards with initial consonants in one pile and the remaining cards in a second pile. Mix up the cards in each pile. Then place a card from the first pile in front of a card from the second pile. Pronounce the sounds on each card separately. Ask children to blend the sounds together to say the word. Do the cards belong together? Keep replacing the onset card until children decide you have a match. As you substitute onsets, ask questions such as the following: "Will we see the *moucans* polishing their beaks?" "No!" "The *sloucans*?" "No!" "The *toucans*?" "Yes!"

Literature Links

The first three books are just right for introducing students to the days of the week; the last two books provide additional information about jungle animals and plants:

Cookie's Week by Cindy Ward (Penguin Putnam, 1997)

Today Is Monday by Eric Carle (Penguin Putnam, 1993)

The Very Hungry Caterpillar by Eric Carle (Penguin Putnam, 1986)

The Great Kapok Tree: A Tale of the Amazon Rain Forest by Lynn Cherry (Harcourt, 1990)

Here Is the Tropical Rain Forest by Madeleine Dunphy (Hyperion, 1997)

Shared Writing

Jungle Fun Big Book: Ask children to pretend they are going to visit the jungle for a week. What fun activities will they do with the animals they meet there? Have children dictate sentences for each day of the week. For example, *On Monday, we swing in the trees with the monkeys. On Tuesday, we eat fruit with the toucans*, and so on. Divide the class into small groups. Have group members work together to copy one of the sentences onto an oversized sheet of paper and then illustrate it. Bind the pages together to create a class big book entitled, "Our Week in the Jungle."

Extending the Poem

Jungle Puppet Show

Children can make a jungle mural to use as a backdrop for a finger puppet show featuring the animals in the poem.

Materials

- ▲ picture books about the rain forest (see Literature Links, left)
- ▲ tempera paint (various colors, including several shades of green and brown)
- ▲ 8-foot-long piece of bulletin board paper
- ▲ paintbrushes
- ▲ finger puppet patterns (page 55)
- ▲ crayons
- ▲ scissors
- ▲ tape

1. Share some of the books with children to give them a better idea of what jungles are like.

2. Together, use the paints to create a mural depicting a jungle scene on the bulletin board paper. Help children paint tall trees, large leaves, dangling vines, and a few brightly colored flowers.

3. Provide each child with a copy of the puppet patterns. Have them color the puppets and cut them out.

4. Show children how to tape together the ends of the bands on the patterns to create puppets that they can slip over their fingers.

5. After your mural has dried, hang it on the wall. Divide the class in half. Have one group of students read the poem aloud as the second group uses the finger puppets to act out the poem in front of the jungle scenery. Allow groups to switch roles.

jaguar

monkey

toucan

parrot

turtle

boa

tree frog

sloth

The Year Goes 'Round

January, the new year starts.

February is full of hearts.

March is windy as can be.

April rains on you and me.

May days are bright and sweet.

June welcomes my bare feet.

July is hot. Where's the shade?

August is time for lemonade.

September school bells start the day.

October leaves all fall away.

November blows the empty trees.

December shines with lights of peace.

Circle-Time Poetry: Math Scholastic Teaching Resources

The Year Goes 'Round

Introducing the Poem

- Write the poem on a sheet of chart paper. Draw symbols related to some of the months around the poem. For example, you may want to draw a heart, an umbrella, a tulip, a leaf, and a candle.

- Invite children to come up with different actions to accompany each line of the poem. Invite them to pretend to blow party horns as you read the first line, trace hearts in the air as you read the second line, whistle like the wind for the third line, and so on.

Talking About the Poem

▲ Ask students if they have ever used a calendar to help them remember a special day or event such as a holiday, a party, or a doctor's appointment. Model how to use a calendar by recording children's birthdays on one. After you've written down each child's birthday, close the calendar. Then say, "I wonder who has a birthday in February? Oh, yes, I can see Jesse's name written right here, February 21st." Continue flipping through the calendar and pointing out birthdays.

▲ Ask children to clap out the syllables in the name of each month to help them segment the words and hear each phoneme. Then write the months on separate sticky notes and randomly distribute them to students. Reread the poem. Pause at the end of each line and repeat the name of the month it highlights. The child who is holding the matching sticky note should then come up to the chart and place it over the name of the month.

Working With Words

Month-by-Month Sequencing Game: Write the name of the 12 months on separate index cards. Punch a hole in the upper right and left corners of each card. Tie string through the holes to make necklaces. Randomly distribute the necklaces to 12 students. Have children put on the necklaces and arrange themselves in order from January to December. Let students refer to the poem for guidance. Repeat the activity until all children have had a chance to participate.

Literature Links

Follow different characters through a year in these lighthearted stories:

One Lighthouse, One Moon by Anita Lobel (Greenwillow, 2000)

A Red Wagon Year by Kathi Appelt (Harcourt, 1996)

Twelve Hats for Lena: A Book of Months by Karen Katz (Simon & Schuster, 2000)

Shared Writing

My Favorite Month Sentences: Write the following sentence frame on the chalkboard several times. Ask children to help you complete the frame by telling you which months of the year are their favorites and why.

My favorite month of the year is _____

because _____.

Extending the Poem

Cupcake Calendar

Make paper birthday cupcakes to give children additional practice naming and sequencing the 12 months of the year.

Materials

▲ cupcake pattern (page 59)   ▲ glue

▲ crayons or markers   ▲ scissors

▲ glitter, sequins, confetti, or ▲ clothespins
  similar decorative materials   ▲ clothesline

❶ Provide each child with a cupcake pattern. Help each child write his or her birthday on the top line. Children can write their name on the bottom line.

❷ Have students use the art materials to decorate the cupcakes.

❸ Help children cut out the cupcakes.

❹ Give each child a clothespin. Explain to children that they are going to attach the cupcakes to the clothesline in month-by-month order, beginning with the current month. For example, if it is September, ask, "Who has a birthday this month?" Have children with September birthdays approach the clothesline. Help them arrange themselves in numerical order according to the day of the month on which their birthdays fall. Then have children attach their cupcakes to the clothesline. Ask, "What month comes after September?" The next batch of students then adds their cupcakes to the line. Continue in this manner until all students have clipped their cupcakes to the clothesline.

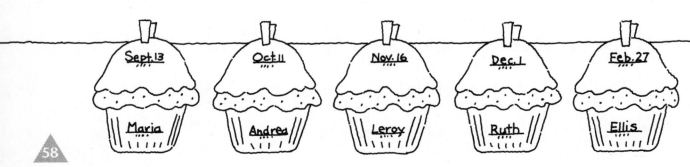

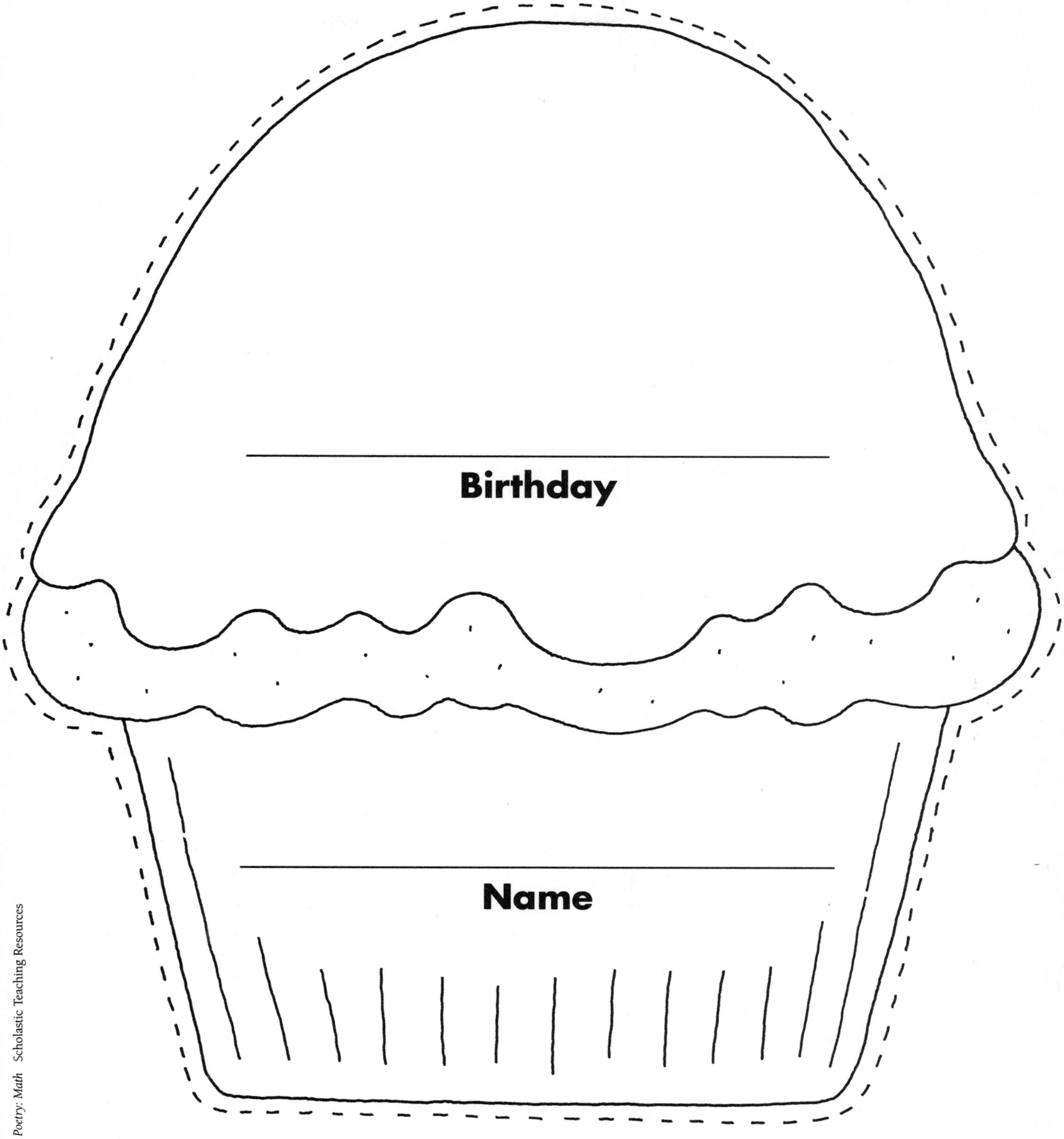

Birthday

Name

Ready, Set, Grow!

Our teacher says we're growing.
She keeps track on the wall.
We let her measure each of us
as we stand up straight and tall.
The pencil marks are rising
as days and weeks go by.
Inch by inch we're growing.
We're reaching for the sky!

Circle-Time Poetry: Math   Scholastic Teaching Resources

Ready, Set, Grow!

Introducing the Poem

◎ Write the poem on a sheet of chart paper. Draw one or more rulers next to the text.

◎ Have children make themselves small by crouching down on the floor. As you read the poem, they can slowly stretch up as they pretend to grow. By the time you read the last line of the poem, children should be standing on their tiptoes and stretching their arms over their heads as if they are reaching for the sky.

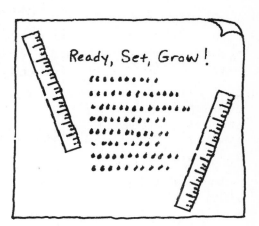

Talking About the Poem

▲ Ask children if they have ever had their height measured at the doctor's office or at home. Does anyone know his or her height? Begin a discussion about the different tools we can use to measure things, such as measuring tapes, rulers, counting cubes, feet, hands, string, and so on. Explain the difference between standard and nonstandard units of measure.

▲ Say the word *measure* several times. Ask students what sound they hear at the beginning of this word. What letter makes this sound? Invite a volunteer to find and circle the word *measure* in the poem. Can they find another word that begins with *m*?

▲ Have volunteers underline all the words ending in *-ing*.

Working With Words

Initial Consonant Pass-Around: Ask students to think of fun things to measure that begin with the letter *m*. Pass a tape measure around the circle and have children pretend to use it as they say what they are measuring. For example, "I am measuring a monkey," "I am measuring a marshmallow," "I am measuring a mountain," and so on.

Shared Writing

Measurement Word Wall: Ask children to brainstorm words related to size and measurement (for example, *big, huge, giant, little, tiny, tall, short, long, wide, narrow, heavy, light, measure, inches, feet, meters, centimeters, ruler, scale*). Write the words students come up with on a sheet of chart paper. Then provide students with index cards. Assign each child a word to copy onto a card. Use the cards to create a word wall on the theme of measurement.

Literature Links

In these books, children use nonstandard units of measure to make size comparisons:

Super Sand Castle Saturday by Stuart J. Murphy (HarperCollins, 1998)

Ten Beads Tall by Pam Adams (Child's Play, 2002)

Extending the Poem

Head-to-Toe Measurements

In this activity, children use a variety of different objects to measure their height.

Materials

▲ bulletin board paper
▲ crayons
▲ various objects for measuring (counting cubes, blocks, paper clips, and so on)
▲ pencils

① Have each child lie down on a sheet of bulletin board paper. Use a crayon to trace the child's outline.

② Allow time for children to experiment using various objects to measure their height.

③ Help children write sentences on the paper about their measurements. For example, "I am 12 blocks tall," "I am 70 counting cubes tall," "I am 56 paper clips tall," and so on.

④ As a further challenge, invite children to use the objects to measure the length of their arms and legs.

If I Measured a Giraffe...

(Sing to the tune of "The Itsy Bitsy Spider")

The itsy bitsy inchworm
climbed up a tall giraffe.
It tickled as it wiggled
and made the creature laugh.
Inch by inch she traveled,
never did she stop.
Up and up and up she went,
until she reached the top!
If I measured a giraffe,
I think that I would ask
the itsy-bitsy inchworm
to help me with the task.

200, 201,
202.....

If I Measured a Giraffe...

Introducing the Poem

🌀 On the left side of a sheet of chart paper, draw a giraffe from the neck up. Draw an inchworm crawling up the giraffe's neck. Write the poem next to the drawing.

🌀 As you sing the poem together, have children move their index fingers so that they look like inchworms crawling. Invite children to "inch" their fingers up through the air as they pretend to climb a giraffe's long neck.

Talking About the Poem

▲ Do students know what the word *task* means? Solicit their ideas before providing the definition. Ask why they think it might be a difficult task to measure a giraffe.

▲ Point out the word *inch* in *inchworm*. How many times do children see the word *inch* in the poem? Do students think inchworms are really an inch long? Show children a ruler and point out how long one inch is. Explain that while some inchworms may be exactly one inch, others may be longer or shorter. People call them inchworms simply because they are very small.

▲ Ask students what sound they hear at the beginning of the word *inchworm*. Reread the poem slowly and have them listen for other words with the short-*i* sound.

Working With Words

Vowel Listening Game: Make enough copies of the inchworm picture-word card on page 66 for each child. Have children color their inchworm, cut the card out, and tape it to a craft stick or drinking straw. Next, read a list of words, some of which feature the short-*i* sound and some of which feature other vowel sounds (for example, *fish, itch, sit, fun, sip, tap*). Tell students that every time they hear a word with the short-*i* sound, they should raise their cards over their heads.

inchworm

Shared Writing

Tall and Long Word Web:
Giraffes are tall animals with long necks. Can students think of other tall and long things for an itsy bitsy inchworm to measure? Make a word web showing their ideas.

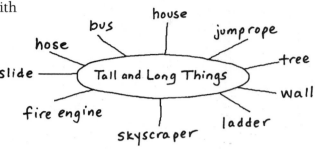

house
bus
jump rope
hose
tree
slide — Tall and Long Things
wall
fire engine
ladder
skyscraper

Literature Links

These stories feature characters who are masters of measuring:

Carrie Measures Up! by Linda Williams Aber (Kane Press, 2001)

Inch by Inch by Leo Lionni (HarperCollins, 1995)

Measuring Penny by Loreen Leedy (Henry Holt, 2000)

Extending the Poem

Itsy-Bitsy Inchworm Ruler

Children make their very own inchworm rulers to practice measuring classroom items.

Materials
▲ inchworm ruler pattern (page 66)   ▲ scissors
▲ cardstock   ▲ tape
▲ crayons   ▲ standard ruler

1 Copy the pattern page onto cardstock and provide each student with a copy.

2 Have children color the two 6-inch pieces of the ruler and cut them out.

3 Then help them tape the segments end-to-end to make one 12-inch ruler.

4 Hold up the standard ruler and show students the one-inch markings. Count out all 12 inches on the ruler. Then hold up the inchworm ruler to compare it to the standard ruler. Point out that the rulers are the same length and that each inchworm is exactly one inch long.

5 Show students how to use their inchworm ruler to measure various classroom items such as crayons, books, desks, and even the neck of the giraffe on the poem page!

6 Allow children time to practice using their rulers. Have them count the number of inches an item is by counting inchworms. Provide several challenges for students. For example, you may want to ask, "Can you find something that is less than three inchworms long? Can you find something that is more than eight inchworms long?" and so on.

7 For fun, have students use their inchworm rulers to show how tall a giraffe is. Take students into the hallway. Have them lay 18 rulers end to end. Tell children that this is how tall some giraffes are!

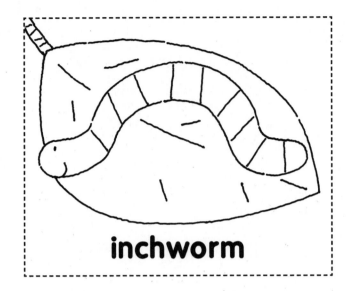

inchworm

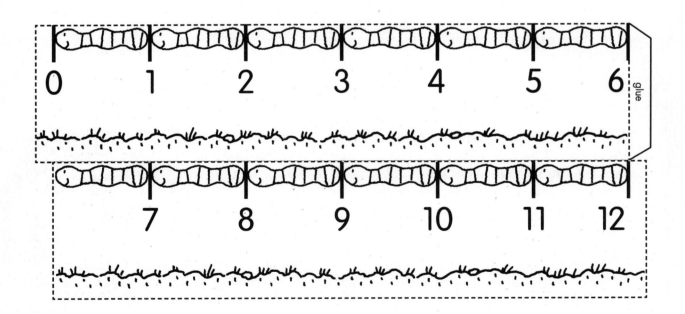

Mixing Up a Snack

We're going on a field trip.
We'd like to take a snack.
Let's mix up a recipe
and put it in our pack.
We'll need a cup of raisins
and chocolate chips to munch.
Let's add a cup of tiny seeds
and yummy nuts for crunch.
We can work together
and use a measuring cup.
We'll measure the ingredients
and soon we'll eat them up!

Mixing Up a Snack

Introducing the Poem

- Draw a large outline of a measuring cup on a sheet of chart paper. Write the poem inside the outline.

- Provide each child with a measuring cup. (Ask parents and other caregivers to send in plastic measuring cups with their child beforehand.) Let students act out the measuring of ingredients by scooping the cups and pouring them in the air as you read the poem together.

Talking About the Poem

▲ Hold up a measuring cup. Explain what the marks and numbers on the cup mean. Ask students why we need measuring cups. Has anyone used a measuring cup at home while helping in the kitchen? Encourage students to share their experiences.

▲ Have volunteers circle the four ingredients named in the poem. Ask children what ingredients they could use instead of these things to make a different snack. Their snack ideas can be serious (for example, cereal, pretzels, goldfish crackers, and banana chips) or silly (for example, noodles, mustard, lemonade, and peas). Write some of students' ideas on sticky notes and place them over the words *raisins, seeds, nuts,* and *chocolate chips.* Reread the poem with students' substitutions.

▲ Use sticky notes to cover the words *pack* in line 4, *crunch* in line 8, and *up* in line 12. Reread the poem and ask children to try to guess the missing words. Provide guidance by pointing out the word each should rhyme with.

Working With Words

Word Family Sack Sort: On separate index cards, write words from the *-ack* word family (for example, *back, black, crack, Jack, Mack, pack, rack, sack, shack, snack, stack, quack, Zack*). Create additional cards for words that do not feature this phonogram—for example, *cat, tap, stick, clock,* and so on. Make sure there is a word card for each child. Mix the cards up and randomly distribute them. Put a large paper bag in the middle of the circle. Tell children you are going to pack a sack of *-ack* words. One by one, have them hold up the word cards. Read each word together. Have children decide if the word is part of the *-ack* family. Ask, "Does it rhyme with *sack*?" If it does, the student holding the card should pack the word in the paper sack. Continue playing until students have packed all the *-ack* words in the sack.

Shared Writing

Snack Time Recipe: Ask students to help you write a recipe for the snack described in the poem. Begin by asking children to think of a name for the snack. Write the name at the top of a piece of chart paper. Then ask students to dictate a list of ingredients and step-by-step directions. Provide guidance as needed.

> **Sweet Crunchy Munchies**
>
> **Ingredients**
>
> 1 cup raisins   1 cup sunflower seeds
> 1 cup chocolate chips   1 cup nuts
>
> **Directions**
> 1. Pour all of the ingredients in a bowl.
> 2. Mix the ingredients together.
> 3. Eat and enjoy!

Literature Links

Here are two books that will help children learn more about measuring volume:

Capacity by Henry Arthur Pluckrose (Scholastic, 1995)

What's Up With That Cup? by Sheila Keenan (Scholastic, 2001)

Extending the Poem

Yummy Snack Crunch

Students practice measuring as they mix up a delicious snack to munch.

Materials

- measuring cups
- container filled with dried beans, rice, popcorn, or birdseed
- plastic containers in various sizes
- large mixing bowl
- cereal
- small pretzels
- chocolate chips
- raisins
- wooden spoon
- small paper cups
- recipe card pattern (page 70)

1. Allow plenty of time for children to use the measuring cups to measure the dried beans or other items into the plastic containers. As they work, ask questions such as, "Can you measure two cups of beans into this container? How many cups of beans do you need to fill that container? Which of these containers will hold more beans?" and so on.

2. After all children have had a chance to experiment with the measuring cups, make a snack together. Invite volunteers to measure two cups each of the cereal, pretzels, chocolate chips, and raisins.

3. Have additional volunteers pour the ingredients into the mixing bowl and stir them together.

4. Serve the snack in the paper cups. (Check with caregivers for any food allergies and provide a substitute snack for those children.)

5. Give each child a copy of the recipe card pattern. At the top, have children write a name for the snack they created. Then help them list the ingredients and write the directions for making it.

Recipe Card Pattern

Ingredients

Directions

Something Heavy, Something Light

We can weigh something heavy.
We can weigh something light.
We can use a balance scale
for weighing things just right.

This scale is like a seesaw
going up and down.
The light side goes up to the sky,
the heavy to the ground.

We can weigh something light,
like a feather or a mouse.
Imagine something heavy,
like an elephant or house!

We can weigh something heavy.
We can weigh something light.
We can use a balance scale
for weighing things just right.

Something Heavy, Something Light

Something Heavy,
Something Light

Introducing the Poem

⊚ Draw a simple balance scale on one side of a sheet of chart paper. Write the poem beside the scale.

⊚ Before reading the poem, show students an actual balance scale and demonstrate how it works.

⊚ Invite children to move their arms up and down like balance scales as you read the poem aloud.

Talking About the Poem

▲ Ask children where they have seen or used scales. Do they get weighed during checkups at the doctor's office? Have they ever seen someone weigh fruit or meat at the supermarket? Why do people weigh things?

▲ Have children pass a feather around the circle. Do they notice how light the feather feels in their hand? Next, pass around a brick. Do students notice how the brick seems to weigh their hand down? Tell children you are going to place the two items on a balance scale. Ask them to predict which object will make the arm of the scale sink, lifting the other object up high? Test their predictions. Did they guess right?

▲ Point out the words *we* and *weigh*. Ask students what sound they hear at the beginning of these words. Have them underline and count all the *w*'s in the poem.

Working With Words

Balance Scale Rhyming Game: Here's a fun way to practice rhyming *and* using a balance scale. To prepare for the game, find pairs of objects whose names rhyme, such as a toy *mouse* and *house*, a *sock* and a *block*, a *duck* and a *truck*, a *goat* and a *boat*, a *cat* and a *hat*, a *pan* and a *man*. Mix up the objects and place them in the center of the circle. Have children take turns finding pairs of objects whose names rhyme. Ask students to guess which object is heavier. Then put the objects on the balance scale to test their predictions.

Shared Writing

Heavy and Light Chart:
Ask children to brainstorm a list of things that are heavy and a list of things that are light. Record their ideas on a chart. Be sure to include the items mentioned in the poem.

Things That Are Heavy	Things That Are Light
elephant	feather
house	mouse
brick	raisin
books	paper clip
gallon of milk	leaf

Literature Links

Reinforce the concept of measuring weight with these resources:

Me and the Measure of Things by Joan Sweeney (Crown, 2001)

Weight by Henry Arthur Pluckrose (Scholastic, 1995)

You Can Use a Balance by Linda Bullock (Children's Press, 2004)

Extending the Poem

Balance Scale Weigh-In

Gather a variety of small objects and let children compare their weights using a balance scale.

Materials

▲ small objects of varying weight (for example, books, coins, crayons, keys, toys, fruit, paper clips, canned foods, game pieces)

▲ chart paper

▲ marker

▲ balance scale

❶ Have a volunteer select two objects from the collection you have gathered. Pass the objects around the circle. Ask students which object they think weighs more. If you put the objects on the scale, which object would go down and which object would go up? Record children's predictions on the chart paper.

❷ Have another volunteer place the objects on the scale. Did students guess correctly? Record the results of the "weigh-in" next to their prediction.

❸ Invite children to continue choosing and weighing objects in this manner. Pose challenges as they experiment with the scale. For example, you might want to ask, "Can you find an object that weighs less than the apple? Can you find an object that weighs more than the crayon? What happens when two objects weigh the same thing?" and so on.

A Graph Is Handy Dandy

We can graph the weather
or animals in the zoo.
We can graph our eye color.
Who has brown or green or blue?
We can graph our pets at home.
Who has dogs and who has cats?
We can graph our winter clothes.
How many mittens, scarves, and hats.
A graph is handy dandy
when you want to show
which is most and which is least.
A graph will let you know.

Circle-Time Poetry: Math   Scholastic Teaching Resources

A Graph Is Handy Dandy

Introducing the Poem

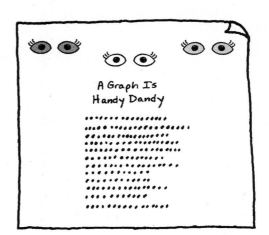

◉ Write the poem on a sheet of chart paper. Draw and color a pair of green eyes, brown eyes, and blue eyes along the top of the page.

◉ Invite children to clap every time they hear the word *graph* as you read the poem aloud.

Talking About the Poem

▲ Ask students if they know what a graph is. Explain that graphs are a kind of picture that give us information about how many there are of one thing compared to another.

▲ To help students grasp the concept of graphing, make a simple graph of eye colors. Precut one-inch squares of brown, blue, and green construction paper. (Add other colors depending on the eye colors of the children in your class.) Have each child take a colored square that corresponds to his or her eye color. Write three labels across the bottom of a sheet of chart paper: *Brown Eyes, Blue Eyes, Green Eyes.* Each child then tapes his or her square above the appropriate label. Have children use the graph to answer simple questions such as, "How many children have brown eyes? Do more children have brown eyes or blue eyes?" and "Do fewer children have green eyes or blue eyes?"

▲ Ask children to find the four pairs of rhyming words in the poem. Have volunteers underline each rhyming pair using a different colored marker.

Working With Words

Rhyming Word Graph: Write the words *zoo, cat,* and *show* from the poem along the bottom of a sheet of chart paper. Challenge students to come up with as many rhymes as they can for each word. Graph the rhyming words on the chart paper. Use the graph to compare the number of rhymes students were able to generate for each word.

blue		
new	hat	
boo	pat	
do	mat	know
flew	fat	go
moo	bat	low
two	rat	mow
who	sat	snow
zoo	**cat**	**show**

Literature Links

The first two resources are informational books that introduce students to different kinds of graphs; the third is a fictional account of how a girl uses a graph to track the sales at her lemonade stand:

Graphs by Bonnie Bader (Penguin, 2003)

Graphs by Sara Pistoia (Child's World, 2002)

Lemonade for Sale by Stuart J. Murphy (HarperCollins, 1997)

Shared Writing

Graph Comparison Sentences: Refer children to the eye color graph you created in the Talking About the Poem activity (page 75). Model how to write sentences summarizing the information on the graph. For example, *Fifteen children have brown eyes. Five children have blue eyes. Ten more children have brown eyes than blue eyes,* and so on. Repeat the activity for the rhyming word graph you created in the Working With Words activity (page 75). This time, invite children to dictate sentences as you write.

Extending the Poem

Favorite Zoo Friends

Which zoo animal does your class like best? Students can create a picture graph to find out.

Materials

▲ marker   ▲ zoo animal patterns (page 77)

▲ chart paper   ▲ tape

❶ Draw a simple five-column graph on the chart paper. Label the columns *Monkeys, Elephants, Lions, Giraffes,* and *Penguins.*

❷ Make several copies of the zoo animal patterns. (Enlarge the animal patterns, if desired.) Cut the animal cards apart and sort them into five separate piles.

❸ Show children a picture of each zoo animal. Ask which of the five is their favorite. They should then take a picture of that animal from the appropriate pile.

❹ Have each child tape the picture he or she chose above the corresponding label on the graph.

❺ Guide children in using the information on the graph to answer questions such as, "Which animal do most children like best? Do more children like lions or monkeys? How many more children chose giraffes than penguins as their favorite animal?" and so on.

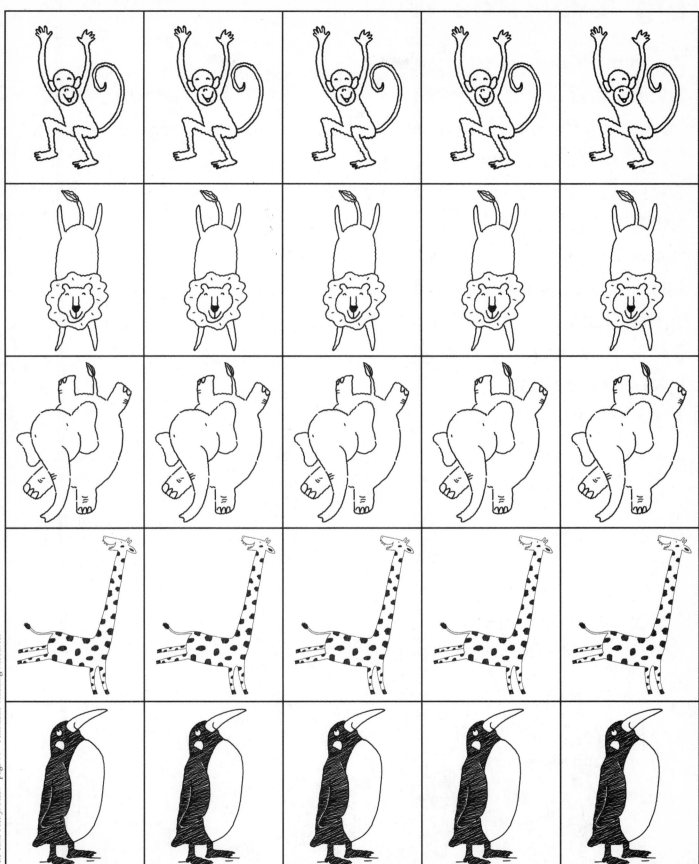

Big Toys, Little Toys

When my toy box is a jumble
and my toys are all a-tumble,
I use my fingers and my eyes
to sort by color, shape, and size.
Some balls are red and some are blue.
There are yellow and green balls, too.
Some blocks are round and some are square.
I'll put the rectangles over there.
Some bears are big and some are small.
Some dolls are short and some are tall.
I put each toy in its pile.
Then I sit and play awhile!

Circle-Time Poetry: Math Scholastic Teaching Resources

Big Toys, Little Toys

Introducing the Poem

⦿ Write the poem on a sheet of chart paper. Draw a few simple toys such as balls, blocks, and teddy bears around the text.

⦿ Glue the chart paper with the poem on it to a large box. Have children fill the box with toys from home. (Ask parents or caregivers beforehand to send in one of their child's favorite toys.)

Talking About the Poem

▲ Ask children to explain what the word *sort* means. Invite them to describe their experiences sorting toys or other items at home or school. Reach into the box and pull out the toys one by one. Lay the toys on the floor. Ask children to think of different ways you can sort the toys. Then invite volunteers to help you organize the toys into piles based on the sorting rules children come up with.

▲ Have volunteers circle all the words in the poem that name colors. Then have volunteers underline all the words that name shapes.

▲ Can children find two pairs of words in the poem that are opposites? Challenge them to come up with other pairs of opposites.

Working With Words

Initial Consonant Toy Sort: Gather some or all of the following toys that begin with the initial consonants *b, c, d, j,* and *p: bear, ball, blocks, boat, bubbles, crayon, cow, car, doll, dinosaur, duck, dog, jump rope, jacks, puzzle,* and *puppet*. Mix up the toys and set them on the floor. Hold up the toys one by one and have children say what they are. Ask what sound they hear at the beginning of each toy's name. Have students sort the toys into separate piles according to their initial consonant sound.

Shared Writing

All-Kinds-of-Toys List Poem: Recognizing different attributes is the first step in classifying objects. Have children write a list poem about the toys in your box that focuses on the toys' various characteristics. Write the phrase *Toys* at the top of a piece of chart paper, then list the attributes students come up with. Write the word *Toys* again at the bottom of the list to complete the poem.

Toys
big toys
small toys
round toys
square toys
loud toys
red toys
blue toys
spotted toys
striped toys
soft toys
fun toys
Toys

Literature Links

The first book is a fictional story in which a girl sorts her toys to clean up her room; the two other books offer factual information about classifying objects:

More or Less a Mess by Sheila Keenan (Scholastic, 1996)

Sets: Sorting Into Groups by Michele Koomen (Capstone Press, 2001)

Sorting by Henry Arthur Pluckrose (Scholastic, 1995)

Extending the Poem

Button, Bean, and Bead Sorts

Try this activity to give students additional practice sorting objects according to different attributes.

Materials

▲ dried beans (various shapes, colors, and sizes)

▲ buttons (various shapes, colors, and sizes)

▲ beads (various shapes, colors, and sizes)

▲ paper

▲ glue

▲ markers

1 Provide each child with a scoop of beans, buttons, or beads and a sheet of paper.

2 Discuss the different ways students can sort the objects. Would they like to sort the objects by color? By shape? By size? Once students have decided upon a sorting rule, they should separate the objects into piles.

3 Have students glue the sorted groups of objects to their paper.

4 Help each child write his or her sorting rule at the top of the paper. Allow time for children to share their work with the rest of the class.

I sorted the buttons by shape.

by Stuart